# CHURCH

### SUPPERS

*p*

This is a Parragon Publishing Book
First published in 2006

Parragon Publishing
Queen Street House
4 Queen Street
Bath BA1 1HE
United Kingdom

Copyright © Parragon Books Ltd 2006

This edition designed by Fiona Roberts
Recipes and photography by
The Bridgewater Book Company Ltd.

ISBN: 1-40547-317-7

Printed in China

NOTE
This book uses metric, imperial, and US cup
measurements. Follow the same units of
measurement throughout; do not mix metric
and imperial. All spoon measurements are
level: teaspoons are assumed to be 5 ml and
tablespoons are assumed to be 15 ml. Unless
otherwise stated, milk is assumed to be full fat,
eggs and individual vegetables such as
potatoes are medium, and pepper is freshly
ground black pepper.

The times given for each recipe are an
approximate guide only because the
preparation times may differ according
to the techniques used by different people and
the cooking times may vary as a result of the
type of oven and other equipment used.

Recipes using raw or very lightly cooked eggs
should be avoided by infants, the elderly,
pregnant women, convalescents and anyone
suffering from an illness. Pregnant and breast-
feeding women are advised to avoid eating
peanuts and peanut products.

# CHURCH SUPPERS

## CONTENTS

# Planning the perfect church supper

Ever since the British settlers first arrived in America, church members have gathered for worship and fellowship. Sharing food has always contributed to the sense of community fostered by church gatherings and church suppers are a wonderful way for all members of the community to meet and spend time together over a meal. Coming together for a meal is an activity that all age groups can participate in, and attending a church supper is something that the whole family can enjoy. Each person, except those that are very young or very old, should contribute something practical to the supper—preparing a dish for the pot luck, supplying flatware, plates, or glasses, helping with serving food, or clearing up after the supper. A supper can be the occasion for a general get together, a gathering to celebrate a specific religious holiday such as Christmas or Easter, or simply an opportunity to welcome new members of the community and help make them feel at home.

Whatever the reason for having a supper, food will be the central element. This book has a range of recipes that have been carefully chosen for the ease with which they can be prepared and served and their universal appeal. There are recipes that will be more suited to summer than winter eating

and vice versa, from light and cool Easy Gazpacho to hearty Lamb Shanks with Cannellini Beans. Informality is the watchword at a church supper—good food, simply prepared and served, with a range of dishes that will appeal to all the family.

If you are asked to organize a church supper, here are some hints and tips that will make things go without a hitch. First, get together a team of helpers to take charge of different aspects of the supper, for example the food and drink, the tables, chairs, dishes and utensils, and any room or table decorations appropriate to the occasion. Make sure that all of those who will be supplying food are asked for the right type of dish—an appetizer or salad, a main course or dessert, a side dish, bread, or biscuits—otherwise you'll end up with an unbalanced menu. Many people have their signature dish, which can become rather too familiar! The recipes in this book will provide plenty of ideas for something different. If the supper is to be pot luck, let people decide what to cook within their allocated category.

Apart from the soups, none of the recipes in this book should be scaled up—if doubling or tripling in size is required, have the same dish cooked by several people. Hot soup should be

prepared on site and should be part of the menu only if your venue has the cooking facilities and utensils for preparing and cooking the quantity required. If the main course is to be a roast meat, such as Traditional Roast Turkey or Roast Ham, decide how much will be needed to feed all the guests and arrange for a pooling of resources.

Arrange for cold dishes to be delivered to the supper venue approximately two hours before the time of the supper—this will provide an opportunity to have them set out. The hot dishes should, if possible, be delivered hot just in time for serving—reheating food is not recommended for reasons of safety.

Make sure that you have enough people to set the venue up in advance of the supper. Children love to help out at these events and there are many little jobs the over-sevens can be given to do (although these should never involve contact with heat or sharp cooking implements). They can wrap eating utensils in napkins and place them in baskets close to where the food will be served; fill dishes with condiments and snacks; butter bread or biscuits; set out glasses and plates.

Avoid the possibility of crowding around the buffet or serving tables by leaving plenty of space between each dish, and clear away one course before serving the next. Make sure that there are plenty of trash cans dotted around so that people can dispose of their own leftovers.

And, finally, don't forget drinks—cold drinks should be kept refrigerated for as long as possible before serving, and there should be plenty of ice available for topping them up.

Breaking bread in communion with others nourishes not just the body but the soul—whatever food is served your table will always be blessed when people come together to eat in fellowship and community.

**FOOD SAFETY**
**Food should be transported either hot or cold (preferably in an insulated container), never at room temperature. If transported hot, it should be served immediately; if it is cold it should be reheated to 165°F/74°C and then kept hot at 140°F/60°C. Food should never be reheated more than once.**

# 1: And to Start...

*Scrumptious soups and salads, delightful dips,*
*and other savory snacks*

 # Chicken Noodle Soup

*1 lb / 450 g skinless, boneless chicken breast, cut*
  *into thin strips*
*5 cups chicken stock*
*⅔ cup heavy cream or panna da cucina*
*salt and pepper*
*4 oz / 115 g dried vermicelli*

*1 tbsp cornstarch*
*3 tbsp milk*
*6 oz / 175 g canned corn*
  *kernels, drained*

Place the chicken in a large pan and pour in the chicken stock and cream. Bring to a boil, then reduce the heat and let simmer for 20 minutes.

Meanwhile, bring a large heavy-bottom pan of lightly salted water to a boil. Add the pasta, return to a boil, and cook for 10–12 minutes, or until just tender but still firm to the bite. Drain the pasta well and keep warm.

Season the soup with salt and pepper to taste. Mix the cornstarch and milk together until a smooth paste forms, then stir it into the soup. Add the corn and pasta and heat through. Ladle the soup into warmed soup bowls and serve.

✿ SERVES 4
✿ PREP TIME 10 MINS
✿ COOKING TIME 25 MINS

# Frankfurter & Split Pea Broth

8 oz/225 g salt belly of pork, cut into cubes

scant 10 cups water

1 lb 2 oz/500 g split peas, soaked in enough
   cold water to cover for 2 hours

4 onions, chopped

2 leeks, chopped

4 carrots, chopped

4 celery stalks, chopped

1 cooking apple, peeled, cored, and chopped

1 tbsp brown sugar

1 bouquet garni

6 frankfurters, cut into
   1-inch/2.5-cm lengths

2 tbsp butter

salt and pepper

celery leaves, to garnish

Put the pork cubes into a large, heavy-bottom pan and add enough cold
water to cover. Bring to a boil over low heat, then drain well. Return the
pork to the pan and add the water.

Drain and rinse the peas, then add them to the pan with the onions,
leeks, carrots, celery, apple, sugar, and bouquet garni. Bring to a boil,
skimming off any scum that rises to the surface. Reduce the heat, cover,
and simmer, stirring occasionally, for 2 hours.

Remove and discard the bouquet garni and stir in the frankfurters and
butter. Season to taste with salt and pepper and heat through. Ladle into
warmed bowls, garnish with celery leaves, and serve immediately.

✿ SERVES 6

✿ PREP TIME 15 MINS +
   2 HRS SOAKING

✿ COOKING TIME 2 HRS 30 MINS

# Beef & Pea Soup

Heat the oil in a large pan over medium heat. Add the onion and garlic and cook, stirring frequently, for 5 minutes, or until softened. Add the bell pepper and carrots and cook for an additional 5 minutes.

Meanwhile, drain the peas, reserving the liquid from the can. Place two-thirds of the peas, reserving the remainder, in a food processor or blender with the pea liquid and process until smooth.

Add the ground beef to the pan and cook, stirring constantly, to break up any lumps, until well browned. Add the spices and cook, stirring, for 2 minutes. Add the cabbage, tomatoes, stock, and puréed peas and season to taste with salt and pepper. Bring to a boil, then reduce the heat, cover, and let simmer for 15 minutes, or until the vegetables are tender.

Stir in the reserved peas, cover, and let simmer for an additional 5 minutes. Ladle the soup into four warmed soup bowls and serve with a bowl of tortilla chips, or some warmed corn or flour tortillas.

❅ SERVES 4
❅ PREP TIME 20 MINS
❅ COOKING TIME 35 MINS

2 tbsp vegetable oil

1 large onion, finely chopped

2 garlic cloves, finely chopped

1 green bell pepper, cored, seeded, and sliced

2 carrots, sliced

14 oz/400 g canned black-eyed peas

1 cup freshly ground beef

1 tsp each ground cumin, chili powder, and paprika

1/4 head of green cabbage, sliced

8 oz/225 g tomatoes, peeled and chopped

2 1/2 cups beef stock

salt and pepper

TO SERVE

tortilla chips, warmed corn tortillas, or flour tortillas

# Easy Gazpacho

*1 small cucumber, peeled and chopped*
*2 red bell peppers, seeded and chopped*
*2 green bell peppers, seeded and chopped*
*2 garlic cloves, coarsely chopped*
*1 fresh basil sprig*
*2½ cups strained tomatoes*
*1 tbsp extra-virgin olive oil*
*1 tbsp red wine vinegar*
*1 tbsp balsamic vinegar*
*1¼ cups vegetable stock*
*2 tbsp lemon juice*
*salt and pepper*

TO SERVE
*2 tbsp diced, peeled cucumber*
*2 tbsp finely chopped red onion*
*2 tbsp finely chopped red bell pepper*
*2 tbsp finely chopped green bell pepper*
*ice cubes*
*4 fresh basil sprigs*
*fresh crusty bread*

Put the cucumber, bell peppers, garlic, and basil in a food processor and process for 1½ minutes. Add the strained tomatoes, olive oil, and both kinds of vinegar and process until smooth.

Pour in the vegetable stock and lemon juice and stir. Transfer the mixture to a large bowl. Season to taste with salt and pepper. Cover with plastic wrap and let chill in the refrigerator for at least 2 hours.

To serve, prepare the cucumber, onion, and bell peppers, then place in small serving dishes or arrange decoratively on a plate. Place ice cubes in 4 large soup bowls. Stir the soup and ladle it into the bowls. Garnish with the basil sprigs and serve with the prepared vegetables and chunks of fresh crusty bread.

- SERVES 4
- PREP TIME 10 MINS + 2 HRS CHILLING
- COOKING TIME 0 MINS

# New England Clam Chowder

2 lb / 900 g live clams
4 bacon strips, chopped
2 tbsp butter
1 onion, chopped

1 tbsp chopped fresh thyme
1 large potato, diced
1¼ cups milk
1 bay leaf

1⅔ cups heavy cream
salt and pepper
1 tbsp chopped fresh parsley

Scrub the clams and put them into a large pan with a splash of water. Cook over high heat for 3–4 minutes until they open. Discard any that remain closed. Strain, reserving the cooking liquid. Set aside until cool enough to handle, reserving 8 for a garnish.

Remove the clams from their shells, chopping them roughly if large, and set aside.

In a clean pan, fry the bacon until browned and crisp. Drain on paper towels and reserve. Add the butter to the same pan, and when it has melted, add the onion. Pan-fry for 4–5 minutes until soft but not colored. Add the thyme and cook briefly before adding the diced potato, reserved clam cooking liquid, milk, and bay leaf. Bring to a boil and simmer for 10 minutes, or until the potato is just tender.

Discard the bay leaf, then transfer to a food processor and blend until smooth, or push through a strainer into a bowl.

Add the clams, bacon, and cream. Simmer for another 2–3 minutes until heated through. Season to taste with salt and pepper. Stir in the chopped parsley and serve, garnished with the reserved clams in their shells.

❄ SERVES 4
❄ PREP TIME 15 MINS
❄ COOKING TIME 30 MINS

# Caesar Salad

*2/3 cup olive oil*

*2 garlic cloves*

*5 slices white bread, crusts removed, cut into*
  *1/2-inch / 1-cm cubes*

*1 large egg*

*2 heads of Romaine lettuce or 3 heads of*
  *Boston lettuce*

*2 tbsp lemon juice*

*salt and pepper*

*8 canned anchovy fillets, drained and coarsely*
  *chopped*

*3/4 cup fresh Parmesan cheese shavings*

Bring a small, heavy-bottom pan of water to a boil.

Meanwhile, heat 4 tablespoons of the olive oil in a heavy-bottom skillet. Add the garlic and diced bread and cook, stirring and tossing frequently, for 4–5 minutes, or until the bread is crispy and golden all over. Remove from the skillet with a slotted spoon and drain on paper towels.

Add the egg to the boiling water and cook for 1 minute, then remove from the pan and set aside.

Arrange the lettuce leaves in a salad bowl.

Mix the remaining olive oil and lemon juice together, then season to taste with salt and pepper. Crack the egg into the dressing and whisk to blend. Pour the dressing over the lettuce leaves, toss well, then add the croutons and anchovies and toss the salad again. Sprinkle with Parmesan cheese shavings and serve.

❋ SERVES 4

❋ PREP TIME 10 MINS

❋ COOKING TIME 10 MINS

# Waldorf Chicken Salad

1 lb 2 oz red dessert apples, diced

3 tbsp fresh lemon juice

2/3 cup light mayonnaise

1 head of celery

4 shallots, sliced

1 garlic clove, finely chopped

3/4 cup walnuts, chopped

1 lb 2 oz/500 g cooked chicken, cubed

1 head of Romaine lettuce

pepper

sliced apple and walnuts, to garnish

Place the apples in a bowl with the lemon juice and 1 tablespoon of mayonnaise. Leave for 40 minutes.

Using a sharp knife, slice the celery very thinly. Add the celery, shallots, garlic, and walnuts to the apple and mix together. Stir in the mayonnaise and blend thoroughly. Add the cooked chicken to the bowl and mix well.

Line a glass salad bowl or serving dish with the lettuce leaves. Pile the chicken salad into the center, sprinkle with pepper, and garnish with the apple slices and walnuts.

❈ SERVES 4

❈ PREP TIME 10 MINS + 40 MINS STANDING

❈ COOKING TIME 0 MINS

# Mexican Tomato Salad

Place the chopped tomatoes and onion slices into a large serving bowl and mix well. Stir in the kidney beans.

Mix the chile, cilantro, olive oil, garlic, and lime juice together in a measuring cup and season to taste with salt and pepper.

Pour the dressing over the salad and toss thoroughly. Serve immediately or cover with plastic wrap and let chile in the refrigerator until required.

❉ SERVES 4
❉ PREP TIME 25 MINS
❉ COOKING TIME 0 MINS

*1 lb 5 oz/600 g tomatoes, peeled, seeded,*
*    and coarsely chopped*
*1 onion, thinly sliced and pushed out*
*    into rings*
*14 oz/400 g canned kidney beans,*
*    drained and rinsed*
*1 fresh green chile, seeded and*
*    thinly sliced*
*3 tbsp chopped fresh cilantro*
*3 tbsp olive oil*
*1 garlic clove, finely chopped*
*4 tbsp lime juice*
*salt and pepper*

# Deviled Eggs

*8 hard-cooked eggs*
*2 tbsp canned tuna*
*4 anchovy fillets*
*6 black olives, pitted*
*1 tsp capers*

Peel the eggs, then cut in half lengthwise and remove the yolks. Mash the yolks, or put in the food processor, along with the tuna, 2 anchovies, 4 olives, and all of the capers.

Blend the ingredients together to make a smooth paste, adding 1 teaspoon of oil from the tuna or anchovies, or some extra-virgin olive oil, to achieve the correct consistency.

Arrange the egg whites on an attractive serving dish. Fill the gaps with the yolk mixture, using either a teaspoon or a piping bag. Make sure the filling is piled high.

Garnish the filled eggs with the remaining anchovies and olives (cut into tiny strips) and serve.

❇ SERVES 4
❇ PREP TIME 10 MINS
❇ COOKING TIME 0 MINS

# Oysters Rockefeller

24 large live oysters

rock salt

3 tbsp butter

6 scallions, chopped

1 large garlic clove, crushed

3 tbsp finely chopped celery

1½ oz/40 g watercress sprigs

1¾ cups baby spinach leaves, rinsed and any tough stems removed

1 tbsp aniseed-flavored liqueur

4 tbsp fresh bread crumbs

few drops of hot pepper sauce, to taste

salt and pepper

lemon wedges, to serve

Preheat the oven to 400°F/200°C. Shuck the oysters, running an oyster knife under each oyster to loosen it from its shell. Pour off the liquor. Arrange a ½–¾-inch/1–2-cm layer of salt in a roasting pan large enough to hold the oysters in a single layer, or use 2 roasting pans. Nestle the oyster shells in the salt so that they remain upright. Cover with a thick, damp dish towel and let chill while you make the topping.

If you don't have oyster plates with indentations that hold the shells upright, line 4 plates with a layer of salt deep enough to hold six shells upright. Set the plates aside.

Melt half the butter in a large skillet over medium heat. Add the scallions, garlic, and celery and cook, stirring frequently, for 2–3 minutes until softened.

Stir in the remaining butter, then add the watercress and spinach and cook, stirring constantly, for 1 minute, or until the leaves wilt. Transfer to a blender or small food processor and add the liqueur, bread crumbs, hot pepper sauce, and salt and pepper to taste. Whiz until well blended.

Spoon 2–3 teaspoons of the sauce over each oyster. Bake in the oven for 20 minutes. Transfer to the prepared plates and serve with lemon wedges.

❈ SERVES 4

❈ PREP TIME 20 – 30 MINS

❈ COOKING TIME 20 MINS

# Warm Crab Dip

This dip tastes best if all the ingredients are mixed together 24 hours in advance to let the flavors develop, but it still tastes good if made just before serving. Put the cream cheese into a bowl and stir in the Cheddar cheese, sour cream, mayonnaise, lemon juice, Worcestershire sauce, and mustard.

Add the crabmeat and salt and pepper to taste and gently stir together. Taste and add extra Worcestershire sauce, if desired. Cover and let chill for up to 24 hours.

When you are ready to heat the dip, remove it from the refrigerator and let it come to room temperature. Meanwhile, preheat the oven to 350°F/180°C. Rub the cut sides of the garlic clove over the base and sides of an ovenproof dish suitable for serving from, then lightly grease. Spoon the crab mixture into the dish and smooth the surface. Heat the dip through in the oven for 15 minutes.

This dip is best kept warm when served, traditionally by using a chafing dish heated by a candle. Either spoon the dip into such a dish, sprinkle with dill, and set over the heat source, or set the dip in its ovenproof dish over a fondue burner and garnish with dill. Serve with savory crackers.

❈ SERVES 8 – 12
❈ PREP TIME 10 MINS +
   24 HRS OPTIONAL CHILLING
❈ COOKING TIME 15 MINS

1¾ cups cream cheese
3 oz/85 g medium Cheddar cheese, grated
1 cup sour cream
4 tbsp mayonnaise
2 tbsp freshly squeezed lemon juice, or to taste
2 tsp Worcestershire sauce, plus extra to taste
2 tsp Dijon mustard
1 lb 2 oz/500 g cooked fresh crabmeat, picked over, or thawed and patted dry if frozen
salt and pepper
1 garlic clove, cut in half
butter, for greasing
fresh dill sprigs, to garnish
savory crackers, to serve

# Guacamole

2 large, ripe avocados

1 lime

2 tsp olive oil

1/2 onion, finely chopped

1 fresh green chile, such as poblano, seeded and finely chopped

1 garlic clove, crushed

1/4 tsp ground cumin

1 tbsp chopped fresh cilantro, plus extra to garnish (optional)

salt and pepper

Cut each avocado in half lengthwise and twist the 2 halves in opposite directions to separate. Stab the pit of each avocado with the point of a sharp knife and lift out.

Peel, then coarsely chop the avocado halves and place in a nonmetallic bowl. Squeeze over the juice of 1 lime and add the oil.

Mash the avocados with a fork until the desired consistency—either chunky or smooth—is reached. Blend in the onion, chile, garlic, cumin, and chopped cilantro, then season to taste with salt and pepper.

Transfer to a serving dish and serve immediately, to avoid discoloration, sprinkled with extra chopped cilantro, if liked, and seasoned to taste with salt and pepper.

❉ SERVES 4
❉ PREP TIME 15 MINS
❉ COOKING TIME 0 MINS

# Tomato Salsa

*3 large, ripe tomatoes*
*½ red onion, finely chopped*
*1 large fresh green chile, such*
  *as jalapeño, seeded and*
  *finely chopped*
*2 tbsp chopped fresh cilantro*
*juice of 1 lime, or to taste*
*salt and pepper*

Halve the tomatoes, scoop out and discard the seeds, and dice the flesh. Place the flesh in a large, nonmetallic bowl.

Add the onion, chile, chopped cilantro and lime juice. Season to taste with salt and pepper and stir gently to combine.

Cover and let chill in the refrigerator for at least 30 minutes to allow the flavors to develop before serving.

✿ SERVES 4 – 6
✿ PREP TIME 10 MINS + 30 MINUTES CHILLING
✿ COOKING TIME 0 MINS

# 2: The Main Event

*A tempting array of favorite meat, fish, and vegetable dishes for the perfect potluck spread*

# Lasagne Al Forno

Preheat the oven to 375°F/190°C. Heat the olive oil in a large, heavy-bottom pan. Add the pancetta and cook over medium heat, stirring occasionally, for 3 minutes, or until the fat starts to run. Add the onion and garlic and cook, stirring occasionally, for 5 minutes, or until softened.

Add the beef and cook, breaking it up with a wooden spoon, until browned all over. Stir in the celery and carrot and cook for 5 minutes. Season to taste with salt and pepper. Add the sugar, oregano, and tomatoes and their can juices. Bring to a boil, reduce the heat, and let simmer for 30 minutes.

Meanwhile, to make the Cheese Sauce, stir the mustard and both cheeses into the hot béchamel sauce.

In a large, rectangular ovenproof dish, make alternate layers of meat sauce, lasagna, and Parmesan cheese. Pour the cheese sauce over the layers, covering them completely, and sprinkle with Parmesan cheese. Bake in the preheated oven for 30 minutes, or until golden brown and bubbling. Serve immediately.

❊ SERVES 4
❊ PREP TIME 15 MINS
❊ COOKING TIME 1 HR 15 MINS

2 tbsp olive oil
2 oz/55 g pancetta or rindless
   lean bacon, chopped
1 onion, chopped
1 garlic clove, finely chopped
1 cup fresh ground beef
2 celery stalks, chopped
2 carrots, chopped
salt and pepper
pinch of sugar
$1/2$ tsp dried oregano
14 oz/400 g canned chopped tomatoes
8 oz/225 g dried no-boil lasagna
   noodles
1 cup freshly grated Parmesan cheese,
   plus extra for sprinkling

CHEESE SAUCE
2 tsp Dijon mustard
$2^1/2$ oz/70 g Cheddar cheese, grated
$2^1/2$ oz/70 g Gruyère cheese, grated
$1^1/4$ cups store-bought béchamel sauce,
   heated through

# Spaghetti & Meatballs

*1 oz/25 g white bread, crusts removed and torn*
 *into pieces*
*2 tbsp milk*
*2 cups fresh ground beef*
*4 tbsp chopped fresh flat-leaf parsley*
*1 egg*
*pinch of cayenne pepper*

*salt and pepper*
*2 tbsp olive oil*
*2/3 cup strained tomatoes*
*7 oz/200 g canned chopped tomatoes*
*1 3/4 cups vegetable stock*
*pinch of sugar*
*1 lb/450 g dried spaghetti*

Place the bread in a small bowl, add the milk and let soak. Meanwhile, place the beef in a large bowl and add half the parsley, the egg, and the cayenne pepper. Season to taste with salt and pepper. Squeeze the excess moisture out of the bread and crumble it over the meat mixture. Mix well until smooth.

Form small pieces of the mixture into balls between the palms of your hands and place on a baking sheet or board. Let chill in the refrigerator for 30 minutes.

Heat the olive oil in a heavy-bottom skillet. Add the meatballs in batches, and cook, stirring and turning frequently, until browned on all sides. Return earlier batches to the skillet, add the strained tomatoes, chopped tomatoes and their can juices, vegetable stock, and sugar, then season to taste with salt and pepper. Bring to a boil, reduce the heat, cover, and let simmer for 25–30 minutes, or until the sauce is thickened and the meatballs are tender and cooked through.

Meanwhile, bring a large, heavy-bottom pan of lightly salted water to a boil. Add the pasta, return to a boil, and cook for 8–10 minutes, or until tender but still firm to the bite. Drain and transfer to a warmed serving dish. Pour the sauce over the pasta and toss lightly. Sprinkle with the remaining parsley and serve immediately.

❀ SERVES 4 – 6
❀ PREP TIME 20 MINS + 30 MINS CHILLING
❀ COOKING TIME 45 MINS

# Meatloaf

*1 thick slice crustless white bread*
*3 cups freshly ground beef, pork, or lamb*
*1 small egg*

*1 tbsp finely chopped onion*
*1 beef bouillon cube, crumbled*
*1 tsp dried herbs*
*salt and pepper*

*TO SERVE*
*tomato or mushroom sauce or gravy*
*mashed potatoes*
*freshly cooked green beans*

Preheat the oven to 350°F/180°C.

Put the bread into a small bowl and add enough water to soak. Let stand for 5 minutes, then drain and squeeze well to get rid of all the water.

Combine the bread and all the other ingredients in a bowl. Shape into a loaf, then place on a cookie sheet or in an ovenproof dish. Put the meatloaf in the oven and cook for 30–45 minutes until the juices run clear when it is pierced with a toothpick.

Serve in slices with your favorite sauce or gravy, mashed potatoes, and green beans.

❉ SERVES 4
❉ PREP TIME 10 MINS
❉ COOKING TIME 45 MINS

# Beef Enchiladas

2 tbsp olive oil, plus extra
   for oiling
2 large onions, thinly sliced
1 lb 4 oz/550 g lean beef, cut
   into bite-size pieces
1 tbsp ground cumin
1/2–1 tsp cayenne pepper
1 tsp paprika
8 soft corn tortillas
8 oz/225 g Cheddar cheese,
   grated

TACO SAUCE
1 tbsp olive oil
1 onion, finely chopped
1 green bell pepper, seeded
   and diced
1–2 fresh hot green chiles,
   seeded and finely chopped
3 garlic cloves, crushed
1 tsp ground cumin
1 tsp ground coriander
1 tsp brown sugar

1 lb/450 g ripe tomatoes,
   peeled and chopped
juice of 1/2 lemon
salt and pepper

❋ SERVES 4
❋ PREP TIME 25 MINS
❋ COOKING TIME 1 HR 10 MINS

Preheat the oven to 350°F/180°C. Oil a large, rectangular baking dish.

To make the Taco Sauce, heat the oil in a deep skillet over medium heat. Add the onion and cook for 5 minutes, or until softened. Add the bell pepper and chiles and cook for 5 minutes. Add the garlic, cumin, coriander, and sugar and cook the sauce for an additional 2 minutes, stirring. Add the tomatoes, lemon juice, and salt and pepper to taste. Bring to a boil, then reduce the heat and let simmer for 10 minutes. Remove from the heat and set aside.

Heat the oil in a large skillet over low heat. Add the onions and cook for 10 minutes, or until soft. Remove with a slotted spoon and set aside. Increase the heat to high, add the beef, and cook, stirring, for 2–3 minutes until browned all over. Reduce the heat to medium, add the spices and salt and pepper to taste, and cook, stirring constantly, for 2 minutes.

Warm each tortilla in a lightly oiled nonstick skillet for 15 seconds on each side, then dip each in the Taco Sauce. Top each with some of the beef and onion mixture and a little grated cheese and roll up. Place seam-side down in the prepared baking dish, top with the remaining Taco Sauce and grated cheese, and bake in the oven for 30 minutes.

# Lone Star Chili

*1 tbsp cumin seeds*

*1 lb 7 oz/650 g rump steak, cut into 1-inch/
   2.5-cm cubes*

*all-purpose flour, well seasoned with salt and
   pepper, for coating*

*3 tbsp beef drippings, bacon fat, or vegetable oil*

*2 onions, finely chopped*

*4 garlic cloves, finely chopped*

*1 tbsp dried oregano*

*2 tsp paprika*

*4 dried red chiles, such as ancho or pasilla,
   crushed, or to taste*

*1 large bottle of South American lager*

*4 squares semisweet chocolate*

Dry-fry the cumin seeds in a heavy-bottom skillet over medium heat, shaking the skillet, for 3–4 minutes, or until lightly toasted. Let cool, then grind in a mortar with a pestle. Alternatively, use a coffee grinder reserved for the purpose.

✿ SERVES 4
✿ PREP TIME 15 MINS
✿ COOKING TIME 2½ – 3½ HRS

Toss the beef in the seasoned flour to coat. Melt the fat in a large, heavy-bottom pan. Add the beef, in batches, and cook until browned on all sides. Remove the beef with a slotted spoon and set aside.

Add the onions and garlic to the pan and cook gently for 5 minutes, or until softened. Add the cumin, oregano, paprika, and chiles and cook, stirring, for 2 minutes. Return the beef to the pan, pour over the lager, then add the chocolate. Bring to a boil, stirring, then reduce the heat, cover, and let simmer for 2–3 hours, or until the beef is very tender, adding more lager if necessary.

# Braised Lamb Shanks with Cannellini Beans

Preheat the oven to 325°F/160°C. Drain the soaked beans and rinse under cold running water. Put in a large pan of cold water, bring to a boil, and skim off any scum, then boil rapidly for 10 minutes. Drain and set aside when boiled.

Meanwhile, heat the oil in a large, flameproof casserole, add the onion, and cook for 5 minutes, or until softened. Add the carrots and celery and cook for a further 5 minutes, or until beginning to soften and the onion is beginning to brown. Add the garlic and cook for a further 1 minute. Push the vegetables to the sides of the pan.

Add the lamb shanks to the pan and cook for about 5 minutes, until browned on all sides. Add the beans to the pan with the tomatoes, wine, and orange zest and juice and stir together. Add the bay leaves and rosemary. Pour in the water so that the liquid comes halfway up the shanks. Season with pepper but do not add salt as this will stop the beans softening.

Bring to a boil, then cover the pan and cook in the oven for about 1 hour. Turn the shanks over in the stock then continue cooking for 1½ hours until the lamb and beans are tender. Remove the bay leaves, then taste and add salt and pepper if necessary. Serve hot, garnished with chopped parsley.

❋ SERVES 4
❋ PREP TIME 25 MINS
❋ COOKING TIME 2½ HRS

9 oz/250 g cannellini beans,
   soaked overnight
2 tbsp sunflower or corn oil
1 large onion, thinly sliced
4 carrots, chopped
2 celery sticks, thinly sliced
1 garlic clove, chopped
4 large lamb shanks
14 oz/400 g canned chopped tomatoes
1⅓ cups red wine
finely pared zest and juice of 1 orange
2 bay leaves
3 rosemary sprigs
scant 1 cup water
salt and pepper
chopped fresh parsley, to garnish

# Spicy Pork & Vegetable Hodgepodge

1 lb/450 g lean boneless pork, cut into
    1-inch/2.5-cm cubes
all-purpose flour, well seasoned with salt and
    pepper, for coating
1 tbsp vegetable oil
8 oz/225 g chorizo sausage, outer casing
    removed, cut into bite-size chunks
1 onion, coarsely chopped
4 garlic cloves, finely chopped
2 celery stalks, chopped
1 cinnamon stick, broken
2 bay leaves

2 tsp allspice
2 carrots, sliced
2–3 fresh red chiles, seeded and finely chopped
6 ripe tomatoes, peeled and chopped
4 cups pork or vegetable stock
2 sweet potatoes, cut into chunks
corn kernels, cut from 1 ear of fresh corn
1 tbsp chopped fresh oregano
salt and pepper
fresh oregano sprigs, to garnish

❖ SERVES 4 – 6
❖ PREP TIME 25 MINS
❖ COOKING TIME 2 HRS

Toss the pork in the seasoned flour to coat. Heat the oil in a large, heavy-bottom pan or ovenproof casserole. Add the chorizo and lightly brown on all sides. Remove the chorizo with a slotted spoon and set aside.

Add the pork, in batches, and cook until browned on all sides. Remove the pork with a slotted spoon and set aside. Add the onion, garlic, and celery to the pan and cook for 5 minutes, or until softened.

Add the cinnamon, bay leaves, and allspice and cook, stirring, for 2 minutes. Add the pork, carrots, chiles, tomatoes, and stock. Bring to a boil, then reduce the heat, cover, and let simmer for 1 hour, or until the pork is tender.

Return the chorizo to the pan with the sweet potatoes, corn, oregano, and salt and pepper to taste. Cover and let simmer for an additional 30 minutes, or until the vegetables are tender. Serve garnished with oregano sprigs.

# Hoppin' John

1 unsmoked ham hock,
  weighing 2 lb 12 oz / 1.25 kg
1 cup dried black-eyed peas,
  soaked overnight in water
  to cover

2 large celery stalks, broken
  in half and tied together
  with a bay leaf
1 large onion, chopped
1 dried red chile (optional)

1 tbsp rendered bacon fat or
  corn or peanut oil
1 cup Carolina long-grain rice
salt and pepper
hot pepper sauce, to serve

Put the ham hock into a large, flameproof casserole with water to cover over high heat. Bring to a boil, skimming the surface. Cover, reduce the heat, and let simmer for 1½ hours.

Stir in the peas, celery bundle, onion, and chile, if using, and let simmer for an additional 1½–2 hours, or until the peas are tender but not mushy and the ham hock feels tender when you prod it with a knife.

Strain the "pot likker" (as the cooking liquid is described in old recipes) into a large bowl and reserve. Set the ham hock aside and set the peas aside separately, removing and discarding the flavorings.

Heat the bacon fat in a pan or flameproof casserole with a tight-fitting lid over medium heat. Add the rice and stir until coated with the fat. Stir in 2 cups of the reserved cooking liquid, the peas, and salt and pepper to taste. (Use the remaining cooking liquid for soup or discard.) Bring to a boil, stirring constantly, then reduce the heat to very low, cover, and let simmer for 20 minutes without lifting the lid.

Meanwhile, cut the meat from the ham hock, discarding the skin and excess fat. Cut the meat into bite-size pieces.

Remove the pan from the heat and let stand for 5 minutes, again without lifting the lid. Fluff up the rice and peas with a fork and stir in the ham, then pile onto a warmed serving platter. Serve with a bottle of hot pepper sauce on the side. Traditional accompaniments include boiled greens and cornbread.

❁ SERVES 4
❁ PREP TIME 10 MINS + 8 HRS
  SOAKING
❁ COOKING TIME 3½ – 4 HRS

# Roast Ham

Place the joint in a large pan, cover with cold water, and gradually bring to a boil over low heat. Cover and let simmer very gently for 1 hour. Preheat the oven to 400°F/200°C.

Remove the ham from the pan and drain. Remove the rind from the ham and discard. Score the fat into a diamond-shaped pattern with a sharp knife.

Spread the mustard over the fat. Mix the sugar and ground spices together on a plate and roll the ham in it, pressing down to coat evenly.

Stud the diamond shapes with cloves and place the joint in a roasting pan. Roast in the oven for 20 minutes until the glaze is a rich golden color.

To serve hot, cover with foil and let stand for 20 minutes before carving. If the ham is to be served cold, it can be cooked a day ahead.

To make a Cumberland Sauce, remove the zest of the oranges using a citrus zester. Place the red currant jelly, port, and mustard in a small pan and heat gently until the jelly has melted. Squeeze the juice from the oranges into the pan. Add the orange zest and season to taste with salt and pepper. Serve cold with the ham. The sauce can be kept in a screw-top jar in the refrigerator for up to 2 weeks.

❄ SERVES 6
❄ PREP TIME 15 MINS +
   20 MINS STANDING
❄ COOKING TIME 1 HR 30 MINS

*1 boneless ham joint,*
  *weighing 3 lb / 1.3 kg*
*2 tbsp Dijon mustard*
*scant 1/2 cup raw sugar*
*1/2 tsp ground cinnamon*
*1/2 tsp ground ginger*
*18 whole cloves*

CUMBERLAND SAUCE
*2 Seville oranges, halved*
*4 tbsp red currant jelly*
*4 tbsp port wine*
*1 tsp mustard*
*salt and pepper*

# Creamed Chicken

4 chicken breast halves or 6 thighs

4 cups water

6 black peppercorns, lightly crushed

1 bay leaf

3 tbsp butter

1 tbsp corn or peanut oil

1 onion, finely chopped

1 red bell pepper, cored, seeded, and chopped

1 green bell pepper, cored, seeded, and chopped

2 tbsp all-purpose flour

1/2 tsp dried thyme

pinch of cayenne pepper, or to taste

salt and pepper

1 1/2 cups heavy cream

7 oz/200 g canned corn kernels, drained

2 tbsp chopped fresh parsley

hot buttermilk biscuits, to serve

❋ SERVES 4 – 6
❋ PREP TIME 20 MINS
❋ COOKING TIME 45 MINS

Put the chicken and water into a large pan over medium-high heat and slowly bring to a boil, skimming the surface. When the gray foam stops rising, reduce the heat to medium, add 1/2 teaspoon of salt, the peppercorns, and bay leaf and let simmer for 20 minutes, or until the chicken is tender and the juices run clear when a skewer is inserted into the thickest part of the meat.

Strain the chicken, reserving about 1 1/4 cups of the cooking liquid. When the chicken is cool enough to handle, remove and discard all the skin and bones and the bay leaf. Cut the flesh into bite-size pieces and set aside.

Melt 2 tablespoons of the butter with the oil in a large skillet over medium-high heat. Add the onion and bell peppers and cook, stirring occasionally, for 5–8 minutes until they are soft but not brown. Remove from the skillet with a slotted spoon and set aside.

Melt the remaining butter in the pan juices. Sprinkle in the flour, thyme, cayenne pepper, and salt and pepper to taste and cook, stirring constantly, for 2 minutes. Slowly stir in the reserved cooking liquid, and continue stirring until no lumps remain. Stir in the cream and bring to a boil. Boil until the sauce is reduced by about half.

Reduce the heat to medium. Stir the chicken into the skillet with the corn, bell peppers, and onion and heat through. Stir in the parsley and adjust the seasoning, if necessary. Serve spooned over hot buttermilk biscuits.

# Chicken Jambalaya

14 oz / 400 g skinless, boneless chicken breast, diced

1 red onion, diced

1 garlic clove, crushed

2¹⁄₂ cups chicken stock

14 oz / 400 g canned chopped tomatoes in tomato juice

generous 1¹⁄₂ cups brown rice

1–2 tsp hot chili powder

¹⁄₂ tsp paprika

1 tsp dried oregano

1 red bell pepper, seeded and diced

1 yellow bell pepper, seeded and diced

¹⁄₂ cup frozen corn kernels

³⁄₄ cup frozen peas

3 tbsp chopped fresh parsley

freshly ground black pepper

crisp green salad, to serve

Put the chicken, onion, garlic, stock, tomatoes, and rice into a large, heavy-bottom pan. Add the chili powder, paprika, and oregano and stir well. Bring to a boil, then reduce the heat, cover, and let simmer for 25 minutes.

Add the red and yellow bell peppers, corn, and peas to the rice mixture and return to a boil. Reduce the heat, cover, and let simmer for an additional 10 minutes, or until the rice is just tender (brown rice retains a "nutty" texture when cooked) and most of the stock has been absorbed but is not completely dry.

Stir in 2 tablespoons of the parsley and season to taste with pepper. Transfer the jambalaya to a warmed serving dish, garnish with the remaining parsley, and serve with a crisp green salad.

❊ SERVES 4

❊ PREP TIME 20 MINS

❊ COOKING TIME 40 MINS

# Southern Fried Chicken

1 chicken, weighing 3 lb 5 oz/1.5 kg,
    cut into 6 or 8 pieces
1/2 cup all-purpose flour
salt and pepper
2–4 tbsp butter
corn or peanut oil, for pan-frying

TO SERVE
A Pot of Southern Peas
Mashed Potatoes

❖ SERVES 4 – 6
❖ PREP TIME 10 MINS +
    4 HRS SOAKING
❖ COOKING TIME 20 – 40 MINS

Put the chicken into a large bowl with 1 teaspoon of salt and cold water
to cover, then cover the bowl and let stand in the refrigerator for at least
4 hours, but ideally overnight. Drain the chicken pieces well and pat
completely dry with paper towels.

Put the flour and salt and pepper to taste into a plastic bag, hold closed,
and shake to mix. Add the chicken pieces and shake until well coated.
Remove the chicken pieces from the bag and shake off any excess flour.

Melt 2 tablespoons of the butter with about 1/2 inch/1 cm of oil in an
ovenproof casserole or large skillet with a lid over medium-high heat.

Add as many chicken pieces as will fit in a single layer without
overcrowding, skin-side down. Cook for 5 minutes, or until the skin is
golden and crisp. Turn the chicken over and cook for an additional
10–15 minutes, covered, until it is tender and the juices run clear when
a skewer is inserted into the thickest part of the meat. Remove the
chicken from the casserole with a slotted spoon and drain well on
paper towels. Transfer to a low oven to keep warm while cooking any
remaining pieces, if necessary, or let cool completely. Remove any
brown bits from the dish and melt the remaining butter in the oil,
adding more oil as needed, to cook the next batch.

# Chicken Stew

*1 chicken, weighing 3 lb 5 oz/
1.5 kg, cut into 6 pieces*
*1 rabbit, dressed, skinned, and
chopped*
*1 bay leaf*
*2 tbsp corn oil*
*2 large onions, finely chopped*
*1 large celery stalk, strings
removed, finely chopped*

*1 lb/450 g juicy, ripe
tomatoes, peeled, seeded,
and chopped*
*2 tbsp tomato paste*
*1 tbsp dried thyme*
*½ tbsp Worcestershire sauce*
*¼ tsp cayenne pepper,
or to taste*
*salt and pepper*

*1 lb/450 g potatoes, peeled
and diced*
*2 large ears of corn, kernels
cut off*
*2 cups shelled fava beans*
*chopped fresh parsley,
to garnish*

Put the chicken and rabbit into a large pan with water to cover by 2 inches/
5 cm over high heat. Bring to a boil, skimming the surface. Reduce the heat,
add the bay leaf and 2 teaspoons of salt and let simmer for 1 hour, or until
both meats are tender and starting to fall off the bones.

Meanwhile, heat the oil in a large, flameproof casserole over medium
heat. Add the onions and celery and cook, stirring frequently, for
3–5 minutes until soft but not browned. Set aside until the chicken
and rabbit are cooked.

Remove the chicken and rabbit pieces from the cooking liquid with a
slotted spoon. When cool enough to handle, remove and discard all the
skin and bones. Cut the flesh into large bite-size pieces and set aside. Pour
5 cups of the cooking liquid into the casserole. Stir in the tomatoes, tomato
paste, thyme, Worcestershire sauce, cayenne pepper, and salt and pepper
to taste, bring to a boil, and boil for 2 minutes. Reduce the heat, add the
potatoes, corn kernels, and fava beans, and let simmer for 20 minutes,
or until the potatoes are tender but not falling apart.

Return the chicken and rabbit to the stew and heat through. Taste and
adjust the seasoning, if necessary. Sprinkle with parsley and serve.

❋ SERVES 4 – 6
❋ PREP TIME 20 MINS
❋ COOKING TIME 1½ HRS

# Traditional Roast Turkey

Preheat the oven to 425°F/220°C. Spoon the dressing into the neck cavity of the turkey and close the flap of skin with a skewer. Place the bird in a large roasting pan and rub all over with 3 tablespoons of the butter. Roast for 1 hour, then lower the oven temperature to 350°F/180°C and roast for an additional 2½ hours. You may need to pour off the fat from the roasting pan occasionally.

Check that the turkey is cooked by inserting a skewer or the point of a sharp knife into the thigh; if the juices run clear, it is ready. Transfer the bird to a carving board, cover loosely with foil, and let rest.

To make the gravy, skim off the fat from the roasting pan then place the pan over medium heat. Add the red wine and stir with a wooden spoon, scraping up the sediment from the bottom of the pan. Stir in the chicken stock. Mix the cornstarch, mustard, vinegar, and water together in a small bowl, then stir into the wine and stock. Bring to a boil, stirring constantly until thickened and smooth. Stir in the remaining butter.

Carve the turkey and serve with vegetables, the dressing, and the gravy.

❀ SERVES 8
❀ PREP TIME 20 MINS
❀ COOKING TIME 3½ HRS

1 turkey, weighing 11 lb/5 kg
4 tbsp butter
5 tbsp red wine
1¾ cups chicken stock
1 tbsp cornstarch
1 tsp French mustard
1 tsp sherry vinegar
2 tsp water

TO SERVE
freshly cooked seasonal vegetables
Store-bought dressing of your choice

# Winter Vegetable Cobbler

*1 tbsp olive oil*

*1 garlic clove, crushed*

*8 small onions, halved*

*2 celery stalks, sliced*

*8 oz/225 g rutabaga, chopped*

*2 carrots, sliced*

*1/2 small head of cauliflower, broken into florets*

*8 oz/225 g mushrooms, sliced*

*14 oz/400 g canned chopped tomatoes*

*1/4 cup red split lentils, rinsed*

*2 tbsp cornstarch*

*3–4 tbsp water*

*1 1/4 cups vegetable stock*

*2 tsp Tabasco sauce*

*2 tsp chopped fresh oregano*

*fresh oregano sprigs, to garnish*

*TOPPING*

*generous 1 1/2 cups self-rising flour*

*pinch of salt*

*4 tbsp butter*

*scant 1 1/4 cups grated aged Cheddar cheese*

*2 tsp chopped fresh oregano*

*1 egg, lightly beaten*

*2/3 cup milk*

❀ SERVES 4
❀ PREP TIME 20 MINS
❀ COOKING TIME 40 MINS

Preheat the oven to 350°F/180°C. Heat the oil in a large skillet and cook the garlic and onions over low heat for 5 minutes. Add the celery, rutabaga, carrots, and cauliflower and cook for 2–3 minutes.

Add the mushrooms, tomatoes, and lentils. Place the cornstarch and water in a bowl and mix to make a smooth paste. Stir into the skillet with the stock, Tabasco, and oregano. Transfer to an ovenproof dish, cover, and bake in the preheated oven for 20 minutes.

To make the topping, sift the flour and salt into a bowl. Rub in the butter, then stir in most of the cheese and the chopped oregano. Beat the egg with the milk in a small bowl and add enough to the dry ingredients to make a soft dough. Knead, then roll out to 1/2-inch/1-cm thick and cut into 2-inch/5-cm circles.

Remove the dish from the oven and increase the temperature to 400°F/ 200°C. Arrange the dough circles around the edge of the dish, brush with the remaining egg and milk mixture, and sprinkle with the reserved cheese. Cook for an additional 10–12 minutes. Garnish with oregano sprigs and serve.

# Fried Catfish Fillets

<table>
<tr><td>

½ cup all-purpose flour

2 eggs

1½ cups yellow cornmeal

½ tsp dried thyme

pinch of cayenne pepper

salt and pepper

</td><td>

2 lb/900 g catfish fillets, skinned, rinsed, and
   patted dry

corn oil, for pan-frying


TO SERVE

Hush Puppies

Coleslaw

</td></tr>
</table>

❋ SERVES 4
❋ PREP TIME 10 MINS
❋ COOKING TIME 4 – 8 MINS
  DEPENDING ON THE SIZE OF
  YOUR PAN

Put the flour onto a plate. Beat the eggs in a wide, shallow bowl. Put the cornmeal onto a separate plate and season with the thyme, cayenne pepper, and salt and pepper to taste.

Dust the catfish fillets with the flour on both sides, shaking off any excess, and dip into the eggs, then pat the cornmeal onto both sides.

Heat about 2 inches/5 cm of oil in a large skillet over medium heat. Add as many catfish fillets as will fit without overcrowding the skillet and cook for 2 minutes, or until the coating is golden brown.

Turn the catfish fillets over and cook for an additional 2 minutes, or until the flesh flakes easily. Remove from the skillet with a slotted spoon and drain on paper towels. Transfer the fillets to a low oven to keep warm while cooking the remaining fillets, if necessary. Add more oil to the skillet as needed.

For a true southern meal, serve the fried catfish with Hush Puppies and Coleslaw. French fries are another popular accompaniment.

# Southwestern Seafood Stew

Preheat the oven to 400°F/200°C. Place the bell pepper quarters, skin-side up, in a roasting pan with the tomatoes, chiles, and garlic. Sprinkle with the dried oregano and drizzle with oil.

Roast in the preheated oven for 30 minutes, or until the bell peppers are well browned and softened.

Remove the roasted vegetables from the oven and let stand until cool enough to handle. Peel off the skins from the bell peppers, tomatoes, and chiles and chop the flesh. Finely chop the garlic.

Heat the oil in a large pan. Add the onion and cook for 5 minutes, or until softened. Add the bell peppers, tomatoes, chiles, garlic, stock, lime rind and juice, chopped cilantro, bay leaf, and salt and pepper to taste. Bring to a boil, then stir in the seafood. Reduce the heat, cover, and let simmer gently for 10 minutes, or until the seafood is just cooked through. Garnish with chopped cilantro before serving.

❀ SERVES 4
❀ PREP TIME 20 MINS +
   10 MINS COOLING
❀ COOKING TIME 50 MINS

*1 each of yellow, red, and orange bell*
  *peppers, seeded and quartered*
*1 lb/450 g ripe tomatoes*
*2 large fresh mild green chiles, such*
  *as poblano*
*6 garlic cloves, peeled*
*2 tsp dried oregano or dried mixed herbs*
*2 tbsp olive oil, plus extra for drizzling*
*1 large onion, finely chopped*
*2 cups fish, vegetable, or chicken stock*
*finely grated rind and juice of 1 lime*
*2 tbsp chopped fresh cilantro, plus*
  *extra to garnish*
*1 bay leaf*
*salt and pepper*
*1 lb/450 g red snapper fillets, skinned*
  *and cut into chunks*
*8 oz/225 g raw shrimp, shelled*
  *and deveined*
*8 oz/225 g cleaned squid, cut into rings*

# Shrimp Gumbo

2 tbsp butter

2 tbsp vegetable oil

9 oz/250 g okra, trimmed and thickly sliced

1 onion, finely chopped

2 celery stalks, quartered lengthwise and diced

1 green bell pepper, seeded
  and diced

2 garlic cloves, very finely chopped

7 oz/200 g canned chopped tomatoes

1/2 tsp dried thyme or oregano

1 fresh bay leaf

salt and pepper

3 1/2 pints chicken stock or water

1 lb/450 g fresh or frozen raw shrimp, shelled
  and deveined

few drops of Tabasco sauce

2 tbsp chopped fresh cilantro, to garnish

Melt the butter with the oil in a large pan over medium heat, add the okra, and cook, uncovered and stirring frequently, for 15 minutes, or until the okra loses its gummy consistency.

Add the onion, celery, bell pepper, garlic, tomatoes, thyme, bay leaf, and salt and pepper to taste. Cover and cook over medium–low heat for 10 minutes.

Pour in the stock. Bring to a boil, then reduce the heat to medium–low, cover, and let simmer for 15 minutes, or until the vegetables are al dente. Add the shrimp and Tabasco sauce and cook for 5 minutes, or until the shrimp turn pink.

Stir in the cilantro to garnish and serve.

❁ SERVES 4
❁ PREP TIME 15 MINS
❁ COOKING TIME 45 MINS

# Boston Fish Pie

2 tbsp butter, plus extra for greasing

2 onions, chopped

2 lb 4 oz/1 kg cod fillet, skinned and cut
    into strips

4 rindless lean bacon strips, cut into
    3 x $^1$/$_2$-inch/3 x 1-cm lengths

2 tbsp chopped fresh parsley

salt and pepper

14 oz/400 g canned great northern beans,
    drained and rinsed

2$^1$/$_2$ cups milk

1 lb 2 oz/500 g potatoes, very thinly sliced

fresh parsley sprigs, to garnish

Preheat the oven to 350°F/180°C. Lightly grease a flameproof casserole with a little butter. Arrange the onions in the bottom and cover with the strips of fish and bacon. Sprinkle with the parsley and season to taste with salt and pepper.

Add the great northern beans, then pour in the milk. Arrange the potato slices, overlapping them slightly, to cover the entire surface of the pie.

Dot the potato slices with the butter. Bake the pie in the oven for 40 minutes, or until the potatoes are crisp and golden. Garnish with parsley sprigs and serve immediately.

✿ SERVES 6

✿ PREP TIME 15 MINS

✿ COOKING TIME 40 MINS

# Tuna-Noodle Casserole

Preheat the oven to 400°F/200°C. Bring a large pan of salted water to a boil. Add the pasta and cook for 2 minutes less than specified on the package instructions.

Meanwhile, melt the butter in a separate, small pan over medium heat. Stir in the bread crumbs, then remove from the heat and set aside.

Drain the pasta well and set aside. Pour the soup into the pasta pan over medium heat, then stir in the milk, celery, bell peppers, half the cheese, and the parsley. Add the tuna and gently stir in so that the flakes don't break up. Season to taste with salt and pepper. Heat just until small bubbles appear around the edge of the mixture—do not boil.

Stir the pasta into the pan and use 2 forks to mix all the ingredients together. Spoon the mixture into an ovenproof dish that is also suitable for serving, and spread out.

Stir the remaining cheese into the buttered bread crumbs, then sprinkle over the top of the pasta mixture. Bake in the oven for 20–25 minutes until the topping is golden. Let stand for 5 minutes before serving straight from the dish.

❋ SERVES 4 – 6
❋ PREP TIME 20 MINS
❋ COOKING TIME 30 – 35 MINS

*7 oz/200 g dried egg ribbon pasta,*
   *such as tagliatelle*

*2 tbsp butter*

*2 oz/55 g fine fresh bread crumbs*

*1¾ cups condensed canned cream*
   *of mushroom soup*

*4 fl oz/125 ml milk*

*2 celery stalks, chopped*

*1 red and 1 green bell pepper, cored,*
   *seeded and chopped*

*5 oz/140 g aged Cheddar cheese,*
   *coarsely grated*

*2 tbsp chopped fresh parsley*

*7 oz/200 g canned tuna in oil, drained*
   *and flaked*

*salt and pepper*

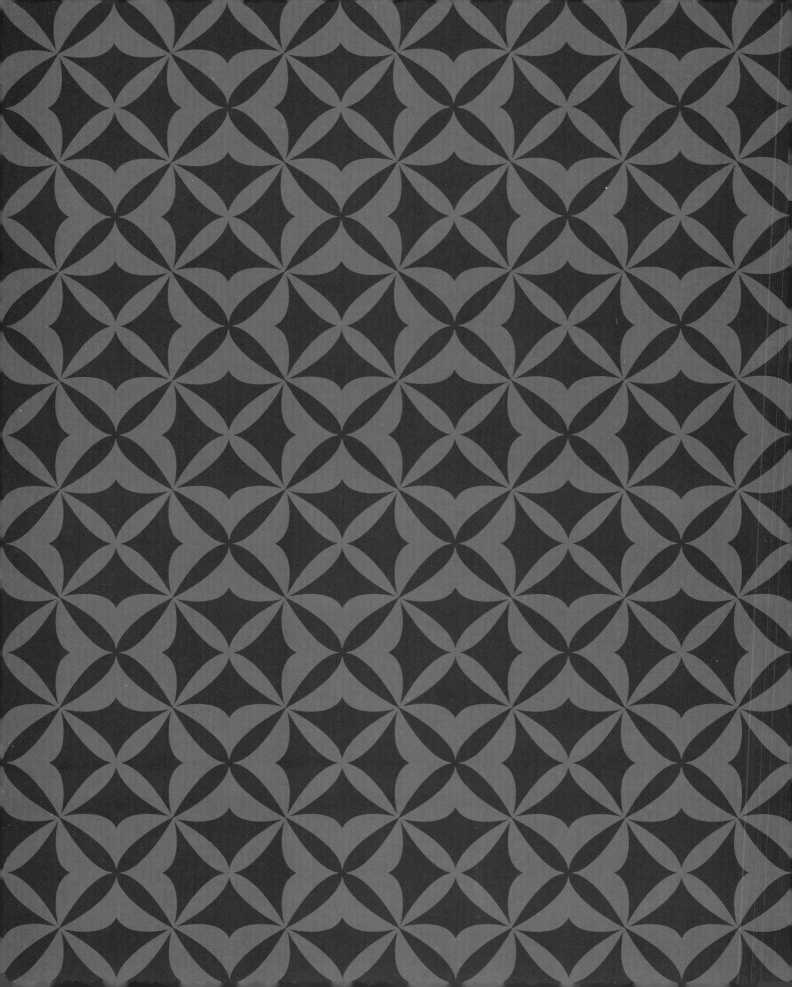

# 3: On the Side

*A mouthwatering mix of delicious and comforting side dishes—the ideal accompaniment*

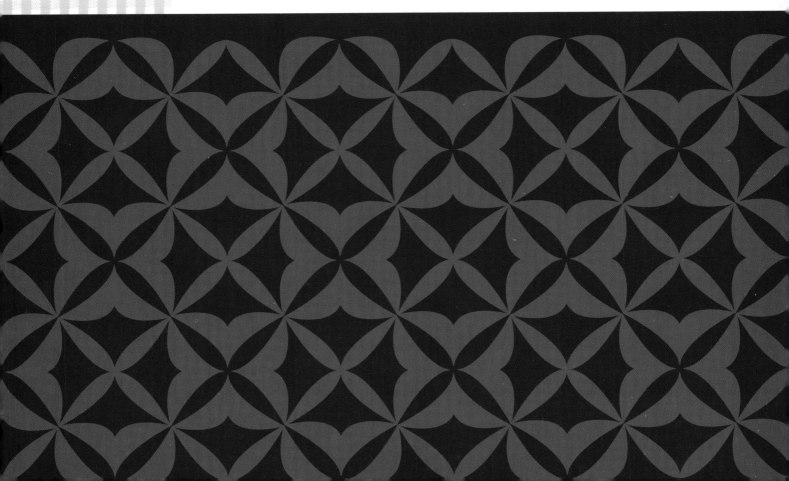

# Macaroni & Cheese

Preheat the oven to 400°F/200°C. Lightly grease a baking dish suitable for serving from. Bring a large pan of salted water to a boil over high heat. Stir in the macaroni and boil for 2 minutes less than the package directions. Drain, rinse under cold running water to prevent further cooking, then drain again and set aside.

Meanwhile, melt 2 tablespoons of the butter in a medium pan over medium heat. Stir into the bread crumbs in a bowl and set aside.

Melt the remaining butter in the same pan. Sprinkle in the flour and stir constantly for 1 minute. Remove the pan from the heat and slowly pour in the milk, whisking constantly.

Return the pan to the heat and simmer, stirring constantly, until the sauce thickens. Remove the pan from the heat and stir in ¾ cup of the Cheddar cheese, ¼ cup of the Gruyère cheese, the nutmeg, cayenne pepper, and salt and pepper to taste, stirring until smooth.

Add the pasta and sliced chiles to the sauce and stir together. Spoon the pasta into the prepared dish and spread out. Sprinkle the remaining cheeses and bread crumbs over the top. Bake in the oven for 25 minutes until golden brown on top.

❉ SERVES 4 – 6
❉ PREP TIME 15 MINS
❉ COOKING TIME 35 MINS

1½ cups dried elbow macaroni
4 tbsp butter, plus extra for greasing
1 cup fine fresh white bread crumbs
1½ tbsp all-purpose flour
1¾ cups warm milk
6 oz/175 g Cheddar cheese, grated
2½ oz/70 g Gruyère cheese, grated
pinch of freshly grated nutmeg
pinch of cayenne pepper
salt and pepper
4 pickled red or green chiles, drained,
    seeded (optional), and sliced

# A Pot of Southern Peas

8 oz / 225 g boneless, rindless belly of pork,
    cut into ½-inch / 1-cm strips
2 large garlic cloves, crushed
1 onion, finely chopped
1 red bell pepper, cored, seeded,
    and finely chopped
1 celery stalk, strings removed,
    finely chopped
1 fresh red chile, seeded and chopped

4 large tomatoes, peeled, seeded,
    and chopped
1 cup water
salt and pepper
1 lb 12 oz / 800 g canned black-eyed peas,
    drained and rinsed
1 tbsp blackstrap molasses
hot pepper sauce, to serve

Put the belly of pork into a deep, dry skillet or pan with a lid over medium–high heat and cook, stirring occasionally, for 10–15 minutes, or until brown and crisp. Remove the pork from the skillet with a slotted spoon and set aside. Pour off all but 1½–2 tablespoons of the rendered fat.

Reduce the heat to medium, stir in the garlic and onion and cook, stirring frequently, for 3–5 minutes, or until the onion is soft. Add the bell pepper, celery, and chile and cook, stirring occasionally, for an additional 3 minutes. Add the tomatoes, water, and pepper to taste and bring to a boil. Reduce the heat, cover, and let simmer for 20 minutes.

Return the pork to the skillet with the peas and molasses and stir to dissolve the molasses. Uncover the skillet and let the beans simmer, stirring occasionally, for 10 minutes, or until most of the liquid has evaporated and the beans are hot. Season to taste and serve with a bottle of hot pepper sauce on the side.

❋ SERVES 4 – 6
❋ PREP TIME 15 MINS
❋ COOKING TIME 45 – 55 MINS

# Boston Beans

*1 lb 2 oz / 500 g dried great
northern beans, soaked
overnight in enough cold
water to cover*

*2 onions, chopped
2 large tomatoes, peeled and
chopped
2 tsp mustard*

*2 tbsp molasses
salt and pepper*

Preheat the oven to 275°F/140°C. Drain the beans and place in a large pan. Add enough cold water to cover, bring to a boil, then reduce the heat and simmer for 15 minutes. Drain, reserving 1¼ cups of the cooking liquid. Transfer the beans to a large casserole and add the onions.

Return the reserved cooking liquid to the pan and add the tomatoes. Bring to a boil, then reduce the heat and simmer for 10 minutes. Remove from the heat, stir in the mustard and molasses, and season to taste with salt and pepper.

Pour the mixture into the casserole and bake in the preheated oven for 5 hours. Serve immediately.

❉ SERVES 8
❉ PREP TIME 10 MINS +
 OVERNIGHT SOAKING
❉ COOKING TIME 5 HRS 30 MINS

# Spicy Potato Wedges

Preheat the oven to 400°F/200°C. Scrub the potatoes, then cut each in half lengthwise and then in half again until you have 8 even-shaped wedges. Put into a large pan of salted water, bring to a boil, and boil for 3 minutes. Drain well and return the wedges to the pan.

Add the oil to the pan and toss the potato wedges in it until coated. Add the paprika, cumin seeds, and turmeric, season to taste with salt and pepper, and mix well together.

Spread the potato wedges out on a baking sheet and bake in the oven for 35–40 minutes until tender and golden brown, turning 2–3 times during cooking. Serve hot, sprinkled with chopped cilantro to garnish.

❋ SERVES 4
❋ PREP TIME 10 MINS
❋ COOKING TIME 40 – 45 MINS

*1 lb 8 oz/675 g large, firm potatoes, such as white or red boiling potatoes, Yukon gold, or russet*
*3 tbsp vegetable oil*
*1 tbsp paprika or 2 tsp ground coriander*
*1 tsp each cumin seeds and turmeric*
*salt and pepper*
*chopped fresh cilantro, to garnish*

# Hush Puppies

1¾ cups yellow cornmeal
½ cup all-purpose flour, sifted
1 small onion, finely chopped
1 tbsp sugar
2 tsp baking powder
½ tsp salt

¾ cup milk
1 egg, beaten
corn oil, for deep-frying

Stir the cornmeal, flour, onion, sugar, baking powder, and salt together in a bowl and make a well in the center.

Beat the milk and egg together in a pitcher, then pour into the dry ingredients and stir until a thick batter forms.

Heat at least 2 inches/5 cm of oil in a deep skillet or pan over high heat until the temperature reaches 350–375°F/180–190°C, or until a cube of bread browns in 30 seconds.

Drop in as many teaspoonfuls of the batter as will fit without overcrowding the skillet and cook, stirring constantly, until the hush puppies puff up and turn golden.

Remove the hush puppies from the oil with a slotted spoon and drain on paper towels. Reheat the oil, if necessary, and cook the remaining batter. Serve hot.

❉ MAKES 36
❉ PREP TIME 10 MINS
❉ COOKING TIME 15 MINS

# Hashed Brown Potatoes

*4 large potatoes*
*1 small onion, finely chopped*
  *(optional)*
*salt and pepper*
*1 large tbsp butter*
*vegetable oil, for pan-frying*
*fresh flat-leaf parsley sprigs,*
  *to garnish*

❉ SERVES 3 – 4
❉ PREP TIME 15 MINS
❉ COOKING TIME 25 MINS

Peel, then coarsely grate the potatoes. Put into a strainer and rinse under cold running water, then let drain for about 15 minutes. Using the back of a wooden spoon, push out any excess water, then wrap the potatoes in a clean dish towel and dry very thoroughly.

Put the potatoes into a large bowl. Add the onion, if using, season to taste with salt and pepper, and mix well together.

Melt the butter with a generous film of oil in a large, heavy-bottom skillet over medium heat. When hot, add the potatoes and toss them several times in the butter and oil, then press down with a spatula and spread evenly over the bottom of the skillet. Press down firmly again. Reduce the heat to low, cover, and cook for 10 minutes, or until the base of the pancake is crisp and golden brown. During cooking, press the pancake down several more times and gently shake the skillet to make sure it isn't sticking.

Using a spatula, cut the pancake into 4 wedges, then carefully turn each wedge. If the bottom of the skillet appears too dry, add a little more oil to prevent the potatoes from sticking. Cook the second side, uncovered, for 15 minutes, or until tender and golden brown. Serve immediately, garnished with parsley sprigs.

 # Mashed Potatoes

Peel the potatoes, placing them in cold water as you prepare the others to prevent them from going brown.

Cut the potatoes into even-sized chunks and cook in a large saucepan of boiling salted water over a medium heat, covered, for 20–25 minutes until they are tender. Test with the point of a knife, but do make sure you test right to the middle to avoid lumps.

Remove the pan from the heat and drain the potatoes. Return the potatoes to the hot pan and mash with a potato masher until smooth.

Add the butter and continue to mash until it is all mixed in, then add the milk (it is better hot because the potatoes absorb it more quickly to produce a creamier texture).

Taste the mashed potatoes and season with salt and pepper as necessary. Serve at once.

❉ SERVES 4
❉ PREP TIME 15 MINS
❉ COOKING TIME 30 MINS

*2 lb/900 g starchy potatoes,*
  *such as russet*
*¼ cup butter*
*3 tbsp hot milk*
*salt and pepper*

# Candied Sweet Potatoes

Bring a large pan of water to a boil over high heat. Add the sweet potatoes and cook for 15 minutes. Drain, then put them under cold running water to cool. When cool enough to handle, peel, then cut each into 8 wedges or chunks. Spread out in the prepared baking dish.

Meanwhile, preheat the oven to 400°F/200°C. Lightly grease a baking dish large enough to hold all the wedges or chunks in a single layer.

Put the butter, sugar, and orange rind and juice into a small pan over medium heat and stir until the sugar dissolves. Bring to a boil and boil until the liquid reduces by about one-third. Stir in the cayenne pepper, if using.

Generously brush the sweet potatoes with the glaze. Bake in the oven, glazing an additional 2–3 times at intervals, for 20–30 minutes, or until the sweet potatoes are tender when pierced with the tip of a knife or a skewer. These are excellent eaten hot or cold.

❋ SERVES 4 – 6
❋ PREP TIME 20 MINS
❋ COOKING TIME 35 – 45 MINS

*3 large orange-fleshed sweet potatoes,*
   *about 9 oz/250 g each, scrubbed*
*2 tbsp butter, melted and cooled,*
   *plus extra for greasing*
*1/4 cup packed brown sugar*
*finely grated rind of 1/2 orange*
*4 tbsp freshly squeezed orange juice*
*pinch of cayenne pepper, or to taste*
   *(optional)*

# Hot Potato Salad

*2 lb 4 oz / 1 kg waxy potatoes*
*2 German-style dill pickles, diced*
*3½ tbsp wine vinegar (red or white)*
*2 tbsp vegetable oil, plus extra for drizzling*
   *(optional)*
*1 onion, finely chopped*

*1–2 garlic cloves, finely chopped*
*1 celery stalk, finely chopped*
*salt and pepper*
*1 tbsp soft light brown sugar*
*1 tbsp German mustard*
*1–2 tbsp chopped fresh parsley*

Peel the potatoes and cut into ½-inch / 1-cm cubes. Bring a large pan of salted water to a boil over high heat. Add the potato cubes and return to a boil. Simmer for 10 minutes, or until just tender, then drain. Do not over-cook.

Turn the potatoes into a large mixing bowl and add the pickles and sprinkle with half the vinegar. Toss lightly.

Heat the oil in a skillet over medium heat. Add the onion and cook for 2–3 minutes, or until just beginning to soften. Add the garlic and celery and cook for 2–3 minutes, stirring frequently. Season to taste with salt and pepper, then stir in the sugar, mustard, and remaining vinegar until the mixture is well blended.

Pour the mixture over the potatoes in the bowl, add the parsley and toss gently to mix. Spoon into a serving bowl and serve warm. If you like, drizzle with a little more oil.

❉ SERVES 4 – 6
❉ PREP TIME 20 MINS
❉ COOKING TIME 25 MINS

 # Coleslaw

8 oz / 225 g white cabbage, cored and grated

8 oz / 225 g carrots, grated

4 tbsp superfine sugar

3 tbsp cider vinegar

salt and pepper

1/2 cup heavy cream

2 pickled green or red bell peppers, drained and
thinly sliced (optional)

4 tbsp finely chopped fresh parsley

Combine the cabbage, carrots, sugar, vinegar, a large pinch of salt, and pepper to taste in a large bowl, tossing the ingredients together. Cover and let chill for 1 hour.

Lightly whip the cream, then gently stir in with the pickled bell peppers, if using, and the parsley. Taste and add extra sugar, vinegar, or salt, if desired. Serve immediately or cover and let chill until required.

❀ SERVES 4 − 6

❀ PREP TIME 15 MINS +
   1 HR CHILLING

❀ COOKING TIME 0 MINS

 # Deep-Fried Okra

Put the okra into a bowl, sprinkle over the water, and gently stir the okra to just moisten.

Put the cornmeal, flour, salt, and pepper to taste into a plastic bag, hold closed, and shake to mix. Add the okra slices to the bag and shake until lightly coated—they won't become completely coated.

Heat at least 2 inches/5 cm of oil in a deep skillet or pan over high heat until the temperature reaches 350–375°F/180–190°C, or until a cube of bread browns in 30 seconds. Add as many okra slices as will fit without overcrowding the skillet and cook, stirring occasionally, for 2 minutes, or until the okra is bright green and the cornmeal coating is golden yellow.

Remove the okra from the oil with a slotted spoon and drain on paper towels. Reheat the oil, if necessary, and cook the remaining okra.

Serve the okra slices hot as a side dish, or serve hot or cold as a snack.

❀ SERVES 4 – 6
❀ PREP TIME 10 MINS
❀ COOKING TIME 10 MINS

*1 lb / 450 g fresh okra, trimmed and cut*
   *into 1/2-inch / 1-cm thick slices*
*about 4 tbsp water*
*1/2 cup yellow cornmeal*
*3 tbsp self-rising or all-purpose flour*
*1/2 tsp salt*
*pepper*
*vegetable oil, for deep-frying*

# Pumpkin Loaf

*vegetable oil, for greasing*

*1 lb/450 g pumpkin flesh*

*½ cup butter, softened, plus extra for greasing*

*¾ cup superfine sugar*

*2 eggs, lightly beaten*

*generous 1½ cups all-purpose flour*

*1½ tsp baking powder*

*½ tsp salt*

*1 tsp ground allspice*

*2 tbsp pumpkin seeds*

Preheat the oven to 400°F/200°C. Grease a 2-lb/900-g loaf pan with oil.

Chop the pumpkin into large pieces and wrap in buttered foil. Cook in the oven for 30–40 minutes until they are tender. Reduce the oven temperature to 325°F/160°C. Let the pumpkin cool completely before mashing well to make a thick paste.

In a bowl, cream the butter and sugar together until light and fluffy. Add the beaten eggs, a little at a time. Stir in the pumpkin paste then sift in the flour, baking powder, salt, and allspice.

Fold the pumpkin seeds gently through the mixture in a figure-eight movement. Spoon the mixture into the prepared loaf pan. Bake in the oven for about 1¼–1½ hours or until a skewer inserted into the center of the loaf comes out clean.

Transfer the loaf to a cooling rack to cool, then serve, sliced and buttered, if wished.

❀ SERVES 6
❀ PREP TIME 1 HR 30 MINS
❀ COOKING TIME 2 HRS 10 MINS

# Chile Cornbread

*scant 1 cup cornmeal*

*scant 1/2 cup all-purpose flour*

*1 tbsp baking powder*

*1 small onion, finely chopped*

*1–2 fresh green chiles, such as jalapeño, seeded*
*and chopped*

*4 tbsp corn or vegetable oil*

*4 1/2 oz / 125 g canned creamed-style corn*
*kernels*

*1 cup sour cream*

*2 eggs, beaten*

Preheat the oven to 350°F/180°C.

Place the cornmeal, flour, and baking powder in a large bowl, then stir in the onion and chiles.

Heat the oil in a 9-inch/23-cm heavy-bottom skillet with a heatproof handle, tipping the skillet to coat the bottom and sides with the oil.

Make a well in the center of the ingredients in the bowl. Add the corn, sour cream, and eggs, then pour in the hot oil from the skillet. Stir lightly until combined. Pour into the hot skillet and smooth the surface.

Bake in the preheated oven for 35–40 minutes, or until a wooden toothpick inserted into the center comes out clean. Cut into wedges and serve warm from the skillet.

❖ SERVES 8

❖ PREP TIME 10 MINS

❖ COOKING TIME 40 – 45 MINS

# Irish Soda Bread

Preheat the oven to 425°F/220°C.

Sift the flour, salt, and baking soda into a mixing bowl.

Make a well in the center of the dry ingredients and pour in most of the buttermilk.

Mix well together using your hands. The dough should be very soft but not too wet. If necessary, add the remaining buttermilk.

Turn the dough out onto a lightly floured surface and knead it lightly. Shape into an 8-inch/20-cm round.

Place the bread on a greased baking tray, cut a cross in the top, and bake in the oven for 25–30 minutes. When done it should sound hollow if tapped on the bottom. Eat while still warm. Soda bread is always best eaten the same day as it is made.

❀ SERVES 4 − 6
❀ PREP TIME 20 MINS
❀ COOKING TIME 30 MINS

*3 cups all-purpose flour*
*1 tsp salt*
*1 tsp baking soda*
*1¾ cups buttermilk*

 # Bacon & Cornmeal Muffins

5¹/₂ oz / 150 g pancetta

generous 1 cup self-rising flour

1 tbsp baking powder

1 tsp salt

generous 1²/₃ cups fine cornmeal

generous ¹/₄ cup golden granulated sugar

3¹/₂ oz / 100 g butter, melted

2 large eggs, beaten

1¹/₄ cups milk

Preheat the oven to 400°F/200°C and preheat the broiler to medium. Line a 12-cup muffin pan with muffin paper liners. Cook the pancetta under the preheated broiler until crisp and then crumble into pieces. Set aside until required.

Sift the flour, baking powder, and salt into a bowl, then stir in the cornmeal and sugar. Place the butter, eggs, and milk in a separate bowl. Add the wet ingredients to the dry ingredients and mix until just blended.

Fold in the crumbled pancetta, then divide the muffin batter between the paper liners and bake in the oven for 20–25 minutes until risen and golden. Remove the muffins from the oven and serve warm, or place them on a cooling rack and let cool.

❈ MAKES 12
❈ PREP TIME 15 MINS
❈ COOKING TIME 30 MINS

# Buttermilk Biscuits

1¾ cups all-purpose flour, plus extra for dusting

1 tbsp superfine sugar

2 tsp baking powder

½ tsp salt

½ tsp baking soda

4 tbsp butter or half butter and half vegetable shortening, diced

⅔ cup buttermilk, plus 1–2 tbsp if needed

a little milk, to glaze

butter, to serve

Preheat the oven to 425°F/220°C. Lightly dust a baking sheet with flour.

Sift the flour, sugar, baking powder, salt, and baking soda into a bowl.

Add the butter, and rub in with the fingertips until coarse crumbs form. Stir in the ⅔ cup of buttermilk and quickly mix into a moist dough with a fork. If dry ingredients remain in the bottom of the bowl, add the extra buttermilk, 1 tablespoon at a time, but do not overmix or the biscuits will be heavy.

Turn the dough out onto a lightly floured counter and very lightly pat out until ¾ inch/2 cm thick. Use a floured 2½-inch/6-cm biscuit or cookie cutter to stamp out 6–7 biscuits, lightly rerolling the trimmings as necessary. To help the biscuits rise while baking, press straight down with the cutter and do not twist it.

Put the biscuits onto the prepared baking sheet and lightly brush the tops with a little milk to glaze. Use the tines of a fork to prick the top of each biscuit in several places.

Bake the biscuits in the oven for 15 minutes, or until they are risen and golden brown on top. Serve at once with plenty of butter.

❖ MAKES 6 – 7
❖ PREP TIME 15 MINS
❖ COOKING TIME 15 MINS

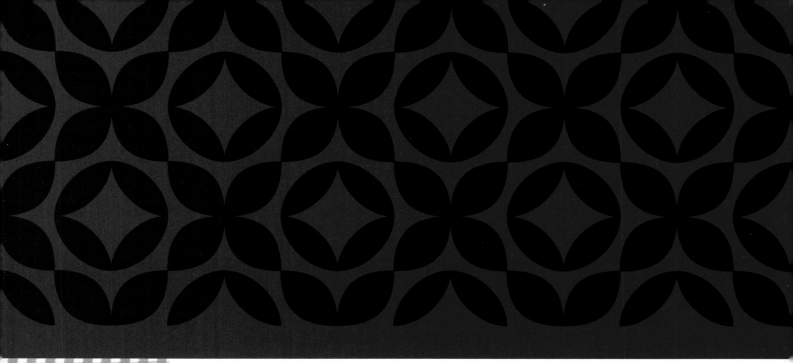

# 4: Sweet Treats

*A marvelous medley of cookies, muffins, pies,
and other goodies for a fantastic finale*

# Classic Oatmeal Cookies

*³/₄ cup butter or margarine,*
*plus extra for greasing*
*1¹/₃ cups packed raw sugar*
*1 egg*
*4 tbsp water*

*1 tsp vanilla extract*
*4¹/₃ cups rolled oats*
*1 cup all-purpose flour*
*1 tsp salt*
*¹/₂ tsp baking soda*

Preheat the oven to 350°F/180°C and grease a large baking sheet.

Cream the butter and sugar together in a large mixing bowl or with an electric mixer. Beat in the egg, water, and vanilla extract until the mixture is smooth.

In a separate bowl, mix the oats, flour, salt, and baking soda. Gradually stir the oat mixture into the butter mixture until thoroughly combined.

Put 30 rounded tablespoonfuls of cookie dough onto the greased cookie sheet, making sure they are well spaced. Transfer to the oven and bake for 15 minutes, or until the cookies are golden brown.

Remove the cookies from the oven and place on a cooling rack to cool before serving.

❈ MAKES 30
❈ PREP TIME 10 MINS
❈ COOKING TIME 15 MINS

# Peanut Butter Cookies

4 oz /115 g butter, softened, plus extra for
    greasing
scant $^1/_2$ cup crunchy peanut butter
generous $^1/_2$ cup golden superfine sugar
generous $^1/_2$ cup brown sugar
1 egg, beaten

$^1/_2$ tsp vanilla extract
$^2/_3$ cup all-purpose flour
$^1/_2$ tsp baking soda
$^1/_2$ tsp baking powder
pinch of salt
$1^1/_2$ cups rolled oats

Preheat the oven to 350°F/180°C, then grease 3 cookie sheets. Place the butter and peanut butter in a bowl and beat together. Beat in the superfine and brown sugars, then gradually beat in the egg and vanilla extract.

Sift the flour, baking soda, baking powder, and salt into the bowl and stir in the oats. Drop spoonfuls of the cookie dough onto the cookie sheets, spaced well apart to allow for spreading. Flatten slightly with a fork.

Bake in the preheated oven for 12 minutes, or until lightly browned. Let cool on the cookie sheets for 2 minutes, then transfer to wire racks to cool completely.

✿ MAKES 26
✿ PREP TIME 20 MINS +
    20 MINS COOLING
✿ COOKING 12 MINS

# Chocolate Chip Cookies

Preheat the oven to 375°F/190°C. Place all the ingredients in a large mixing bowl and beat until they are thoroughly combined.

Lightly grease 2 cookie sheets. Place tablespoonfuls of the mixture onto the cookie sheets, spacing them well apart to allow for spreading during cooking.

Bake in the oven for 10–12 minutes until the cookies are golden brown.

Using a spatula, transfer the cookies to a cooling rack to cool completely before serving.

❉ MAKES 18
❉ PREP TIME 35 MINS
❉ COOKING TIME 10 – 12 MINS

*1½ cups all-purpose flour, sifted*
*1 tsp baking powder*
*½ cup soft margarine*
*scant ⅔ cup light brown sugar*
*¼ cup superfine sugar*
*½ tsp vanilla extract*
*1 egg*
*⅔ cup semisweet chocolate chips*

# Cinnamon Raisin Rolls

**DOUGH**

3¹/₂ cups strong bread flour, plus extra
   for dusting
1 tsp salt
3 tbsp sugar
1 tsp active dry yeast
3 tbsp vegetable shortening, diced
1 egg, lightly beaten
¹/₂ cup warm milk
¹/₂ cup warm water

**FILLING**

¹/₂ cup sugar
4 tbsp granulated light brown sugar
1 tsp ground cinnamon
3 oz/85 g butter, softened, plus extra
   for greasing
2 oz/55 g raisins or golden raisins
¹/₂ cup chopped walnuts or pecans

✽ MAKES 24
✽ PREP TIME 30 MINS +
  2 HRS 45 MINS PROOFING
✽ COOKING TIME 15 – 18 MINS

Sift the flour, salt, and sugar into a medium bowl and stir in the yeast. Stir in the shortening and make a well in the center. Beat the egg, milk, and water together in a separate bowl until well blended. Add to the well and stir into the flour mixture until a soft dough forms. Turn out onto a lightly floured work surface. Knead for 5–7 minutes, or until smooth and elastic.

Oil a large bowl, add the dough, and turn to coat to prevent a crust forming. Cover with a dish towel. Leave to rise in a warm place for 1¹/₂–2 hours, or until doubled in size. Turn out and knead lightly to deflate. Prepare the filling. Combine the sugars and cinnamon in a small bowl.

Generously grease 2 x 12-cup muffin or bun pans. Roll the dough into a large rectangle slightly less than ¹/₄ inch/5 mm thick. Cut vertically in half. Spread the butter over both dough pieces. Sprinkle the sugar mixture evenly over the dough, then sprinkle with the fruit and nuts.

Starting at one long side, tightly roll each piece into a long loaf shape. Lay seam-side down. Cut into 1-inch/2.5-cm slices in one downward movement. Arrange each spiral in a muffin or bun pan. Cover with the dish towel and leave to rise again in a warm place for 30–45 minutes. Preheat the oven to 400°F/200°C. Bake for 15–18 minutes, or until puffed and golden. Remove to a wire rack to cool. Serve warm.

# Lowfat Blueberry Muffins

*vegetable oil cooking spray, for oiling (if using)*
*scant 1½ cups all-purpose flour*
*1 tsp baking soda*
*¼ tsp salt*
*1 tsp allspice*
*generous ½ cup superfine sugar*
*3 large egg whites*

*3 tbsp lowfat margarine*
*⅔ cup thick, lowfat plain or blueberry-flavored yogurt*
*1 tsp vanilla extract*
*¾ cup fresh blueberries*

Preheat the oven to 375°F/190°C. Spray a 12-cup muffin pan with vegetable oil cooking spray, or line it with 12 muffin paper liners. Sift the flour, baking soda, salt, and half of the allspice into a large mixing bowl. Add 6 tablespoons of the superfine sugar and mix together.

In a separate bowl, whisk the egg whites together. Add the margarine, yogurt, and vanilla extract and mix together well, then stir in the fresh blueberries until thoroughly mixed. Add the fruit mixture to the flour mixture and then gently stir together until just combined. Do not overstir the batter—it is fine for it to be a little lumpy.

Divide the muffin batter evenly between the 12 cups in the muffin pan or the paper liners (they should be about two-thirds full). Mix the remaining sugar with the remaining allspice, then sprinkle the mixture over the muffins. Transfer to the oven and bake for 25 minutes, or until risen and golden. Remove the muffins from the oven and serve warm, or place them on a cooling rack and let cool.

❋ MAKES 12
❋ PREP TIME 15 MINS
❋ COOKING TIME 25 MINS

# Chocolate Chip Brownies

Preheat the oven to 350°/180°C. Grease a 9-inch/23-cm square baking pan and line with parchment paper.

Place the chocolate and softened butter in a heatproof bowl set over a pan of simmering water. Stir until melted, then let cool slightly.

Sift the flour into a separate bowl and stir in the superfine sugar.

Stir the beaten eggs into the chocolate mixture, then pour the mixture into the flour and sugar and beat well. Stir in the pistachios and white chocolate, then pour the mixture into the pan, using a spatula to spread it evenly.

Bake in the preheated oven for 30–35 minutes, or until firm to the touch around the edges. Let cool in the pan for 20 minutes. Turn out onto a wire rack. Dust the brownie with confectioners' sugar and let cool completely. Cut into 12 pieces and serve.

❖ MAKES 12
❖ PREP TIME 25 MINS +
   30 MINS COOLING
❖ COOKING TIME 30 – 35 MINS

*1 cup butter, softened,*
   *plus extra for greasing*
*5¹/₂ oz/150 g semisweet chocolate,*
   *broken into pieces*
*generous 1¹/₂ cups self-rising flour*
*scant ²/₃ cup superfine sugar*
*4 eggs, beaten*
*²/₃ cup shelled pistachios, chopped*
*3¹/₂ oz/100 g white chocolate,*
   *coarsely chopped*
*confectioners' sugar, for dusting*

# Cinnamon Streusel Coffeecake

STREUSEL

1 cup pecans or walnuts, chopped

1–2 tsp ground cinnamon

3–4 tbsp sugar

CAKE

scant 1 cup all-purpose flour

1½ tsp baking powder

½ tsp baking soda

4 oz/115 g unsalted butter or margarine, softened, plus extra for greasing

½ cup sugar

3 eggs, lightly beaten, at room temperature

12 fl oz/350 ml sour cream

1 tsp vanilla extract

confectioners' sugar, for dusting

❋ SERVES 10 – 12
❋ PREP TIME 30 MINS +
  30 MINS COOLING
❋ COOKING TIME 50 – 55 MINS

Preheat the oven to 350°F/180°C. Grease a 10-inch/25-cm fluted cake pan. Combine the streusel ingredients in a small bowl. Sift the flour, baking powder and baking soda into a medium bowl.

Put the butter and sugar into a large bowl and, using an electric mixer, beat on low speed until combined. Continue beating on medium speed for 2 minutes, or until pale and fluffy. Gradually add the beaten eggs, about a tablespoon at a time, beating until smooth.

Beat in the flour mixture and sour cream, alternately in 3 batches on low speed until combined, then beat in the vanilla; do not over-beat.

Spoon a little over one-third of the batter into the pan, tilting to distribute evenly. Sprinkle with half the streusel mixture. Drop about one-third more of the batter by tablespoonfuls over the streusel mixture, carefully spreading to just cover. Sprinkle with the remaining streusel mixture. Drop the remaining batter over, spreading to just cover the streusel mixture. Tap the pan gently to knock out any air bubbles and even the mixture.

Bake for 50–55 minutes, or until puffed and golden and a fine knife inserted comes out clean. Remove to a wire rack. Leave to cool for 5–7 minutes. Run a knife around the edge of the pan and carefully ease the cake onto the rack. Serve at room temperature, dusted with confectioners' sugar.

 # Pecan Pie

PIE DOUGH

*generous 1¹/₂ cups all-purpose*
  *flour*
*pinch of salt*
*4 oz/115 g butter, cut into*
  *small pieces*
*1 tbsp lard or vegetable*
  *shortening, cut into*
  *small pieces*

*generous ¹/₄ cup golden*
  *superfine sugar*
*6 tbsp cold milk*

FILLING

*3 eggs*
*generous 1 cup dark brown*
  *sugar*
*1 tsp vanilla extract*

*pinch of salt*
*3 oz/85 g butter, melted*
*3 tbsp corn syrup*
*3 tbsp molasses*
*2 cups shelled pecans, roughly*
  *chopped*
*pecan halves, to decorate*
*whipped cream or vanilla ice*
  *cream, to serve*

❁ SERVES 8
❁ PREP TIME 30 MINS +
  30 MINS CHILLING
❁ COOKING TIME 1 HR

To make the pie dough, sift the flour and salt into a mixing bowl and rub in the butter and lard with the fingertips until the mixture resembles fine bread crumbs. Work in the superfine sugar and add the milk. Work the mixture into a soft dough. Wrap the dough and let chill in the refrigerator for 30 minutes.

Preheat the oven to 400°F/200°C. Roll out the pie dough and use it to line a 9–10-inch/23–25-cm tart pan. Trim off the excess by running the rolling pin over the top of the tart pan. Line with parchment paper, and fill with dried beans. Bake in the oven for 20 minutes. Take out of the oven and remove the paper and dried beans. Reduce the oven temperature to 350°F/180°C. Place a baking sheet in the oven.

To make the filling, place the eggs in a bowl and beat lightly. Beat in the dark brown sugar, vanilla extract, and salt. Stir in the butter, syrup, molasses, and chopped nuts. Pour into the pastry shell and decorate with the pecan halves.

Place on the heated baking sheet and bake in the oven for 35–40 minutes until the filling is set. Serve warm or at room temperature with whipped cream or vanilla ice cream.

# Traditional Apple Pie

To make the pie dough, sift the flour and salt into a large bowl. Add the butter and fat and rub in with the fingertips until the mixture resembles fine bread crumbs. Add the water and gather the mixture together into a dough. Wrap the dough and let chill in the refrigerator for 30 minutes.

Preheat the oven to 425°F/220°C. Roll out almost two-thirds of the pie dough thinly and use to line a deep 9-inch/23-cm pie plate or pie pan.

Mix the apples with the sugar and spice and pack into the pastry shell; the filling can come up above the rim. Add the water if needed, particularly if the apples are a dry variety.

Roll out the remaining pie dough to form a lid. Dampen the edges of the pie rim with water and position the lid, pressing the edges firmly together. Trim and crimp the edges.

Use the trimmings to cut out leaves or other shapes to decorate the top of the pie, dampen and attach. Glaze the top of the pie with beaten egg or milk, make 1–2 slits in the top, and place the pie on a baking sheet.

Bake in the preheated oven for 20 minutes, then reduce the temperature to 350°F/180°C and bake for a further 30 minutes, or until the pastry is a light golden brown. Serve hot or cold, sprinkled with sugar.

❉ SERVES 6
❉ PREP TIME 30 MINS +
    30 MINS CHILLING
❉ COOKING TIME 50 MINS

PIE DOUGH
scant 2 1/2 cups all-purpose flour
pinch of salt
3 oz/85 g butter or margarine, cut into
    small pieces
3 oz/85 g lard or vegetable shortening,
    cut into small pieces
about 6 tbsp cold water
beaten egg or milk,
    for glazing

FILLING
1 lb 10 oz–2 lb 4 oz/
    750 g–1 kg cooking apples, peeled,
    cored, and sliced
scant 2/3 cup packed brown or superfine
    sugar, plus extra for sprinkling
1/2–1 tsp ground cinnamon, allspice, or
    ground ginger
1–2 tbsp water (optional)

# Peach Cobbler

FILLING

6 peaches, peeled and sliced

4 tbsp superfine sugar

$^1/_2$ tbsp lemon juice

$1^1/_2$ tsp cornstarch

$^1/_2$ tsp almond or vanilla extract

vanilla or pecan ice cream, to serve

PIE TOPPING

scant $1^1/_4$ cups all-purpose flour

generous $^1/_2$ cup superfine sugar

$1^1/_2$ tsp baking powder

$^1/_2$ tsp salt

3 oz/85 g butter, diced

1 egg

5–6 tbsp milk

Preheat the oven to 425°F/220°C. Place the peaches in a 9-inch/23-cm square ovenproof dish that is also suitable for serving. Add the sugar, lemon juice, cornstarch, and almond extract and toss together. Bake the peaches in the oven for 20 minutes.

Meanwhile, to make the topping, sift the flour, all but 2 tablespoons of the sugar, the baking powder, and salt into a bowl. Rub in the butter with the fingertips until the mixture resembles bread crumbs. Mix the egg and 5 tablespoons of the milk in a pitcher, then mix into the dry ingredients with a fork until a soft, sticky dough forms. If the dough seems too dry, stir in the extra tablespoon of milk.

Reduce the oven temperature to 400°F/200°C. Remove the peaches from the oven and drop spoonfuls of the topping over the surface, without smoothing. Sprinkle with the remaining sugar, return to the oven, and bake for an additional 15 minutes, or until the topping is golden brown and firm—the topping will spread as it cooks. Serve hot or at room temperature with ice cream.

❀ SERVES 4 – 6
❀ PREP TIME 20 MINS
❀ COOKING TIME 35 MINS

# Upside-Down Cake

1 cup unsalted butter

1/4 cup brown sugar

14–16 hazelnuts

1 lb 5 oz/600 g canned
   apricot halves, drained

3/4 cup turbinado sugar

3 eggs, beaten

1 1/4 cups self-rising flour

1/3 cup ground hazelnuts

2 tablespoons milk

cream, to serve

Preheat the oven to 350°F/180°C.

Grease a 10-inch/25-cm cake pan and line the base with parchment paper.

Cream 1/4 cup of the butter with the brown sugar and spread over the base of the pan.

Place a hazelnut in each apricot half and invert onto the base. The apricots should cover the whole surface.

Cream the turbinado sugar together with the remaining butter until pale and fluffy, then beat in the eggs gradually. Fold in the flour and the ground hazelnuts together with the milk and spread the mixture over the apricots.

Bake in the center of the oven for about 45 minutes until golden brown and well risen. Run a knife around the edges of the pan and invert onto a warm serving plate. Serve warm with the cream.

❋ SERVES 6 – 8
❋ PREP TIME 20 MINS
❋ COOKING TIME 45 MINS

# Mississippi Mud Pie

To make the pie dough, sift the flour and cocoa into a mixing bowl. Rub in the butter with the fingertips until the mixture resembles fine bread crumbs. Stir in the sugar and enough cold water to mix to a soft dough. Wrap the dough and let chill in the refrigerator for 15 minutes.

Preheat the oven to 375°F/190°C. Roll out the dough on a lightly floured counter and use to line a 9-inch/23-cm loose-bottom tart pan or ceramic pie dish. Line with parchment paper and fill with dried beans. Bake in the oven for 15 minutes. Remove from the oven and take out the paper and beans. Bake the pastry shell for an additional 10 minutes.

To make the filling, beat the butter and sugar together in a bowl and gradually beat in the eggs with the cocoa. Melt the chocolate and beat it into the mixture with the light cream and the chocolate extract.

Reduce the oven temperature to 325°F/160°C. Pour the mixture into the pastry shell and bake for 45 minutes, or until the filling has set gently.

Let the mud pie cool completely, then transfer it to a serving plate, if you like. Cover with the whipped cream.

Decorate the pie with chocolate flakes and curls and then let chill until ready to serve.

❀ SERVES 8
❀ PREP TIME 30 MINS +
   COOLING/CHILLING
❀ COOKING TIME 1 HR 10 MINS

PIE DOUGH

generous 1 1/2 cups all-purpose flour,
   plus extra for dusting
2 tbsp unsweetened cocoa
5 oz/140 g butter
2 tbsp superfine sugar
1–2 tbsp cold water

FILLING

6 oz/175 g butter
scant 1 3/4 cups packed brown sugar
4 eggs, lightly beaten
4 tbsp unsweetened cocoa, sifted
5 1/2 oz/150 g semisweet chocolate
1 1/4 cups light cream
1 tsp chocolate extract

TO DECORATE

scant 2 cups heavy cream, whipped
chocolate flakes and curls

# Sweet Potato Pie

To make the pie dough, sift the flour, salt, and sugar into a bowl. Add the butter and vegetable shortening to the bowl and rub in with the fingertips until fine crumbs form. Sprinkle over 2 tablespoons of the water and mix with a fork until a soft dough forms. Add ½ tablespoon of water if the dough is too dry. Wrap in plastic wrap and chill for at least 1 hour.

Meanwhile, bring a large pan of water to a boil over high heat. Add the sweet potatoes and cook for 15 minutes. Drain, then cool them under cold running water. When cool, peel, then mash. Put the sweet potatoes into a separate bowl and beat in the eggs and sugar until very smooth. Beat in the remaining ingredients, except the whipped cream, then set aside until required.

When ready to bake, preheat the oven to 425°F/220°C. Roll out the dough on a lightly floured counter into a thin 11-inch/28-cm circle and use to line a 9-inch/23-cm pie plate, about 1½ inches/4 cm deep. Trim off the excess dough and press the floured tines of a fork around the edge.

Prick the base of the pastry shell all over with the fork and place crumpled kitchen foil in the center. Bake in the oven for 12 minutes, or until lightly golden.

Remove the pastry shell from the oven, take out the foil, pour the filling into the shell, and return to the oven for an additional 10 minutes. Reduce the oven temperature to 325°F/160°C and bake for a further 35 minutes, or until a knife inserted into the center comes out clean. Let cool on a cooling rack. Serve warm or at room temperature with whipped cream.

❉ SERVES 8 – 10
❉ PREP TIME 30 MINS + 1 HR CHILLING
❉ COOKING TIME 1 HR

PIE DOUGH

1¼ cups all-purpose flour, plus extra for dusting
½ tsp salt
¼ tsp superfine sugar
1½ tbsp butter, diced
3 tbsp vegetable shortening, diced
2–2½ tbsp ice-cold water

FILLING

1 lb 2 oz/500 g orange-fleshed sweet potatoes, scrubbed
3 extra-large eggs, beaten
½ cup packed brown sugar
1½ cups canned evaporated milk
3 tbsp butter, melted
2 tsp vanilla extract
1 tsp ground cinnamon
1 tsp ground nutmeg or freshly grated nutmeg
½ tsp salt
freshly whipped cream, to serve

# Index